BRIGHT IDEA BOOKS

LIN-MANUEL
Miranda

by Penelope S. Nelson

CAPSTONE PRESS
a capstone imprint

Bright Idea Books are published by Capstone Press
1710 Roe Crest Drive, North Mankato, Minnesota 56003
www.mycapstone.com

Library of Congress Cataloging-in-Publication Data
Names: Nelson, Penelope, 1994- author.
Title: Lin-Manuel Miranda / by Penelope S. Nelson.
Description: North Mankato, Minnesota : Capstone Press, [2019] | Series:
   Influential people | Includes bibliographical references and index.
Identifiers: LCCN 2018019503 (print) | LCCN 2018021789 (ebook) | ISBN
   9781543541694 (ebook) | ISBN 9781543541298 (hardcover : alk. paper)
Subjects: LCSH: Miranda, Lin-Manuel, 1980- Hamilton--Juvenile literature. |
   Hamilton, Alexander, 1757-1804--Drama--Juvenile literature.
Classification: LCC ML3930.M644 (ebook) | LCC ML3930.M644 N45 2019 (print) |
   DDC 782.1/4092 [B] --dc23
LC record available at https://lccn.loc.gov/2018019503

Editorial Credits
Editor: Mirella Miller
Designer: Becky Daum
Production Specialist: Craig Hinton

J-B
MIRANDA
461-1979

Quote Source
p. 4, "Watch Lin-Manuel Miranda's 2016 Tony Awards Sonnet: 'Love Is Love Is Love Is Love.'" *Mic
Network*, June 12, 2016

TABLE OF CONTENTS

CHAPTER 1

HAMILTON
Is a Hit

"We live through times when hate and love seem stronger," said Lin-Manuel Miranda. He was accepting a **Tony Award**. It was for his musical *Hamilton*. He wanted his speech to be inspiring. He said, "Love is love."

Miranda's musical was a winner! It won 11 awards that night. The cast performed on stage. They sang a song from the show. They danced in costume.

Miranda is known for his inspiring speeches and performances.

Miranda got the idea for the musical from a book. He read a **biography** about Alexander Hamilton. Hamilton was one of the Founding Fathers of the United States.

Hamilton (pictured) worked under George Washington.

Miranda thought everyone could relate to Hamilton's life. He had grown up poor. He worked hard. Later he became successful. Miranda thought rap artists' lives were like this.

WORKING HARD

People told Miranda that *Hamilton* would fail. He did not believe them. He worked hard on every song. Some songs took one year to write!

In the Heights was Miranda's first Broadway project.

Miranda decided to write about Hamilton. Miranda wanted to do something special. He wrote a hip-hop musical. Most musicals have pop, rock, or jazz music. Hip-hop is a newer type of music. Miranda's musical *In the Heights* was also hip-hop style.

Miranda and the cast of *Hamilton* performed at the Tony Awards in 2016.

Miranda worked on the show for a long time. He took years to write it. It told the history of the United States. He used rap music. People of color were in the show. He wanted everyone to connect with the story. Miranda would play Hamilton.

OPENING NIGHT

Hamilton opened in 2015. Audiences loved it. The show was a smash hit!

Crowds gathered everywhere the show went.

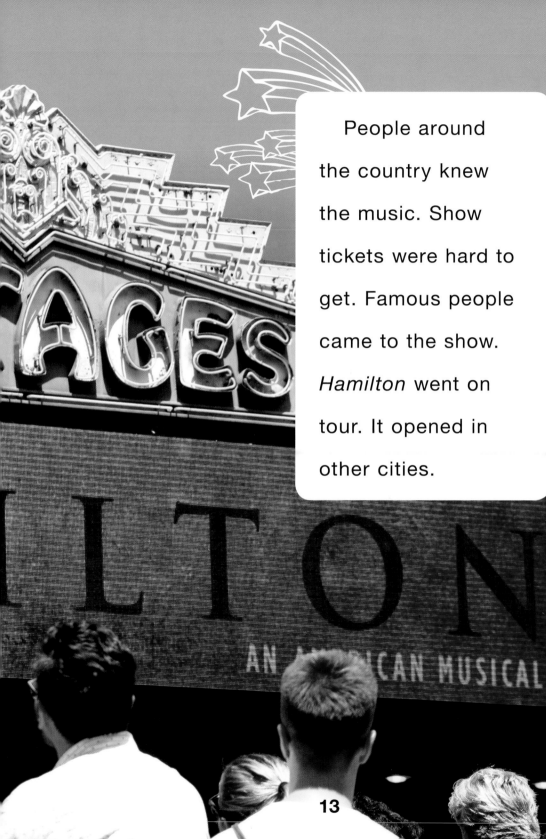

People around the country knew the music. Show tickets were hard to get. Famous people came to the show. *Hamilton* went on tour. It opened in other cities.

CHAPTER 2

GROWING UP
Musical

Lin-Manuel Miranda grew up in New York City. His parents came from Puerto Rico. Many people around him were **immigrants**.

Miranda wanted a career in theater. He liked show tunes and hip-hop. He liked music that told a story. He acted in plays in high school. His parents thought he should be a lawyer. But he followed his own path to success.

Miranda's family is Hispanic.

WRITING HIS FIRST SHOW

Miranda wrote about his neighborhood in his first musical. *In the Heights* was the name of the show. Miranda started writing it in college. He studied and started acting. He was in movies and television shows. Miranda also had other jobs. He was a substitute teacher. He wrote ads. He continued to work hard on his show.

In the Heights won four Tony Awards.

PERSONAL LIFE

Miranda is married to Vanessa Nadal. They met in high school. They have two sons.

Miranda worked with a writing partner on *In the Heights*. They got feedback on the show. It got even better. *In the Heights* opened on **Broadway** in 2008. Miranda acted in the lead role.

Miranda enjoys acting in the musicals he writes.

CHAPTER 3

LIFE AFTER
Hamilton

Miranda worked on *Hamilton* after *In the Heights*. *Hamilton* made Miranda a big star! Many people wanted to work with him. Miranda wrote music for the Disney movie *Moana*. It was a big hit in 2016.

He put together a **mixtape**. Artists sang songs from *Hamilton*. They recorded the selections in their own styles. Miranda sang some songs on the mixtape too. They were songs that he wrote for *Hamilton*. But they did not end up in the final musical.

Miranda attended the *Moana* opening with members of his family.

GIVING BACK

Miranda used his fame to help people. He started the Immigrants: We Get the Job Done **Coalition**. It raised money. The money would help Hispanic people in the United States. It funded groups that provide **social services**. He used social media to help. Famous people shared videos singing songs from *Hamilton*. They asked people to give money.

Miranda performed
with Jennifer Lopez
to raise money.

Then Hurricane Maria hit Puerto Rico in 2017. Miranda wanted to help. He raised money for the country. He wrote a song for Puerto Rico. The money he made from the song went to help the country.

Miranda works to help many different causes.

Miranda has new projects. He is
working on more movies and music.
He is writing music for Disney.
He wrote songs for a live version of
The Little Mermaid.

Miranda (center) films a scene from *Mary Poppins Returns*.

MORE MOVIE PROJECTS

Miranda's next movie was *Mary Poppins Returns*. He acted in the movie.

GLOSSARY

biography
a book that tells the story
of a person's life

Broadway
a theater district in New York
City where many famous
shows are performed

coalition
a group of people joined
together for a common goal

immigrant
a person who moves from
one country to another

mixtape
a collection of music from
many artists

social service
a service that benefits
communities, such as medical
care, education, and housing

Tony Award
a prize given to a musical
or play each year

TIMELINE

1980: Lin-Manuel Miranda is born.

2002: Miranda graduates from Wesleyan University with a degree in theater.

2008: Miranda reads a biography of Alexander Hamilton on vacation.

2008: *In the Heights* opens on Broadway.

2010: Miranda marries Vanessa Nadal.

2015: *Hamilton* opens on Broadway.

2016: Miranda writes music for the Disney movie *Moana*.

ACTIVITY

WRITE YOUR OWN MUSICAL

Lin-Manuel Miranda wrote his first musical about his neighborhood. If you were going to write a musical about the people in your life, what would it include? What things from your neighborhood would you want other people to see? What people in your life would make good characters on Broadway? Think about your life. How could you turn it into a musical or play? Write a scene from that show.

FURTHER RESOURCES

Love learning about Lin-Manuel Miranda? Learn more in these books:

Kramer, Barbara. *Lin-Manuel Miranda: Award-Winning Musical Writer.* Minneapolis: Abdo Publishing, 2017.

Kraus, Stephanie. *Lin-Manuel Miranda.* Huntington Beach, CA: Teacher Created Materials, 2017.

Morlock, Theresa. *Lin-Manuel Miranda: Award-Winning Actor, Rapper, Writer, and Composer.* New York: PowerKids Press, 2018.

Ready to find out more about Broadway and *Hamilton*? Check out these websites:

Broadway Musicals and Plays
https://www.broadway.com

Hamilton: The Musical
http://hamiltonmusical.com/new-york

INDEX